Math on the Job
Serving Your Community
This could be you!

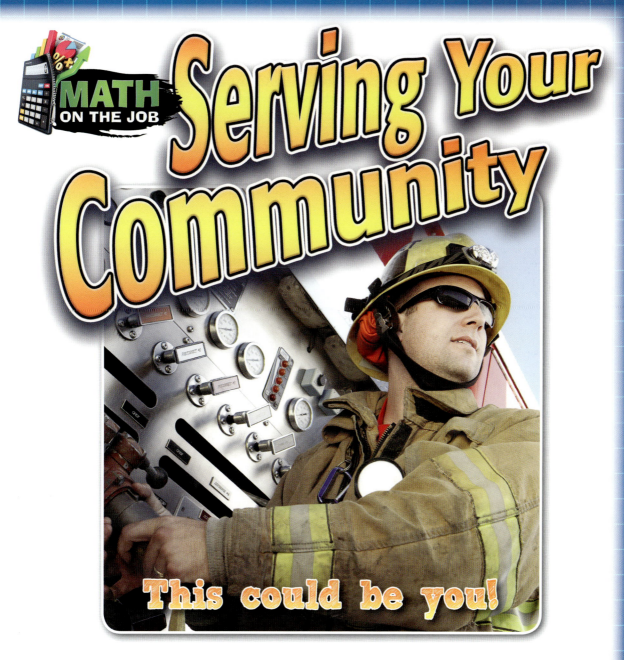

Rick Wunderlich

Crabtree Publishing Company
www.crabtreebooks.com

Crabtree Publishing Company
www.crabtreebooks.com

Dedicated by Rick Wunderlich
To my wife Virginia. Thank you for being my best friend.

Author: Rick Wunderlich

Editorial director: Kathy Middleton

Editors: Reagan Miller, Janine Deschenes, and Kathy Middleton

Photo research: Margaret Amy Salter, Hayley Alguire

Proofreader: Crystal Sikkens

Designer: Margaret Amy Salter

Production coordinator and prepress technician: Margaret Amy Salter

Print coordinator: Katherine Berti

Math consultant: Diane Dakers

Special thanks to Bill Reiach

Photographs:
Shutterstock: © Rihardzz: front cover (top right);
© Guillermo Pis Gonzalez: front cover (bkgd);
© Philipe Ancheta: p6; © silvergull: p10 (top left);
© photocagiao: p11 (middle right); © Rob Wilson: p12;
© Prometheus72: p14;
Wikimedia Commons: p5

All other images by Shutterstock

Library and Archives Canada Cataloguing in Publication

Wunderlich, Rick, author
          Math on the job : serving your community / Richard Wunderlich.

(Math on the job)
Includes index.
Issued in print and electronic formats.
ISBN 978-0-7787-2360-8 (bound).--ISBN 978-0-7787-2366-0 (paperback).--ISBN 978-1-4271-1741-0 (html)

          1. Hazardous occupations--Juvenile literature. 2. Mathematics--Juvenile literature. I. Title. II. Title: Serving your community.

HD7262.W86 2016   j510   C2015-908044-4
                                        C2015-908045-2

Library of Congress Cataloging-in-Publication Data

Names: Wunderlich, Richard, author.
Title: Math on the job. Serving your community / Richard Wunderlich.
Other titles: Serving your community
Description: Series: Math on the job | Includes index. | Description based on print version record and CIP data provided by publisher; resource not viewed.
Identifiers: LCCN 2015046328 (print) | LCCN 2015045155 (ebook) | ISBN 9781427117410 (electronic HTML) | ISBN 9780778723608 (reinforced library binding : alk. paper) | ISBN 9780778723660 (pbk. : alk. paper)
Subjects: LCSH: Mathematics--Juvenile literature. | Hazardous occupations--Juvenile literature.
Classification: LCC HD7262 (print) | LCC HD7262 .W86 2016 (ebook) | DDC 510--dc23
LC record available at http://lccn.loc.gov/2015046328

Printed in Canada/022016/IH20151223

Crabtree Publishing Company
www.crabtreebooks.com   1-800-387-7650

Copyright © **2016 CRABTREE PUBLISHING COMPANY.** All rights reserved. No part of this publication may be reproduced, stored in a retrieval system or be transmitted in any form or by any means, electronic, mechanical, photocopying, recording, or otherwise, without the prior written permission of Crabtree Publishing Company. In Canada: We acknowledge the financial support of the Government of Canada through the Canada Book Fund for our publishing activities.

Published in Canada
Crabtree Publishing
616 Welland Ave.
St. Catharines, ON
L2M 5V6

Published in the United States
Crabtree Publishing
PMB 59051
350 Fifth Avenue, 59th Floor
New York, New York 10118

Published in the United Kingdom
Crabtree Publishing
Maritime House
Basin Road North, Hove
BN41 1WR

Published in Australia
Crabtree Publishing
3 Charles Street
Coburg North
VIC 3058

Contents

Serving your Community 4
Career 1: Coast Guard Commander 6
Think Like a Coast Guard Commander 7
Math Toolbox: Time and Distance 13
Career Pathways: Coast Guard Commander 14
Career 2: Firefighter 15
Math Toolbox: Patterns in Numbers 20
Career Pathways: Firefighter 21
Career 3: Police Officer 22
Think Like a Police Officer 23
Math Toolbox: Pie Charts 28
Career Pathways: Police Officer 29
Learning More & Career 1 Answers 30
Glossary & Career 2 Answers 31
Index, Author's Bio, Career 2 & 3 Answers . 32

Please note:
The standard and metric systems are used interchangeably throughout this book.

Serving Your Community

There are many brave, well-educated, and well-trained men and women who work in careers that serve their communities. Whether they are rescuing people caught in a hurricane, saving people trapped inside a burning building, or finding out the cause of a traffic accident, these workers are committed to making their communities safer places to live and work.

Many communities around the world are built along coastlines because close access to water makes transportation easier. The Coast Guard is in charge of enforcing the law and ensuring the safety of people on the water and the environment, as well as managing search and rescue operations. The Coast Guard is responsible for the safety and security of vessels and people, from the icy waters of the Arctic, where oil tankers, cruise ships, and fishing boats travel, to the parts of the oceans filled with **oil rigs** and boats for personal use and recreation.

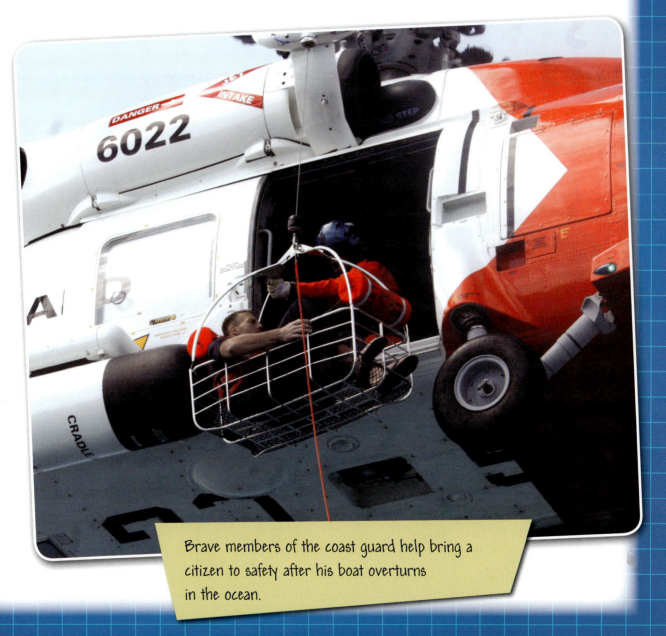

Brave members of the coast guard help bring a citizen to safety after his boat overturns in the ocean.

CAREER 1

COAST GUARD COMMANDER

The Coast Guard includes a number of wonderful careers, such as helicopter pilot, radar operator, security personnel, ship officers, aircraft crew, and, of course, the very exciting career as a Coast Guard commander.

Coast Guard commanders may be in charge of different **units**, including helicopter pilots and rescue boats. Commanders need to make sure the helicopter pilots are well organized and trained, because in order to do their jobs, they must often fly in terrible weather or dangerously close to huge ships. They risk their lives attempting rescues and arresting smugglers and other criminals, while at the same time ensuring that ships and boats are operating safely and legally. They protect our coastlines and the people and vessels that operate along them.

During emergency events, such as hurricanes, the Coast Guard is often called on to rescue people caught in storms. A Coast Guard commander may be responsible for directing helicopter crews to the areas where they are most needed. Helicopter pilots race to areas where people are in need. People may be trapped on top of homes or buildings surrounded by flood waters or struggling to stay afloat. The helicopter pilot lowers rescue crews from their hovering helicopters to reach victims and pull them to safety. What an exciting and rewarding career!

Think Like a Coast Guard Commander

Suppose a hurricane has created massive flooding over a wide area on the east coast of North America.

Your unit is called to rescue victims trapped on rooftops in the city where your Coast Guard base is located.

The water is so high on city streets that it is very tough to use street addresses to find victims. Your first job is to organize the Coast Guard personnel into **squads**, including helicopter crews.

Hurricanes often bring flooding and very high winds to coastal lands. It is not unusual for Coast Guard personnel to have to risk their lives to save people during storms.

SOLVE:

1 Suppose there is an emergency, and you have 90 personnel under your command in the Coast Guard. You need to divide them into 30 squads to cover the entire emergency area. How many personnel would be in each squad?

2 a) Of the 90 personnel, one-third of them have extra first-aid training. How many of the personnel have extra first-aid training?

b) If each squad is given the same number of personnel with extra first-aid training, how many would each squad have?

3 You are responsible for a rectangular section of the city that is 12 miles long and 10 miles wide.

a) What is the area, in square miles, you are responsible for? (Hint: Area = length x width)

b) What is the perimeter, or total distance around the section? Perimeter is found by adding the length of each side together.

FACTS:

When rescuing flood victims, your reaction time is extremely important. Victims can quickly drown in rising waters, get washed away by raging streams, or become so cold waiting that they become hypothermic, which can cause their body systems to shut down. A Coast Guard commander must get his or her personnel to the flood victims as quickly as possible.

You look at a map. You realize that you can use the pattern of the street grid of houses to direct your squads, even if the streets are under water. In this city, there is an average of eight city blocks per mile, all built in a similar layout.

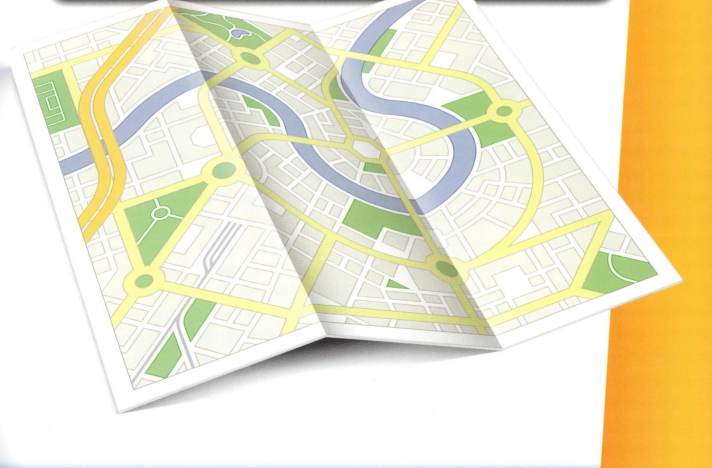

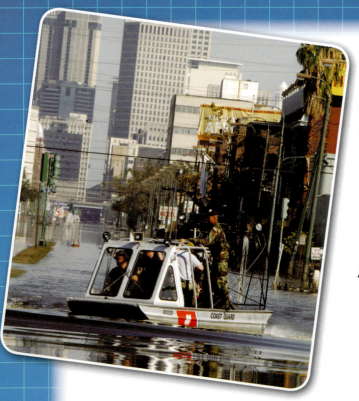

ANALYZE:

1 To reach some victims, squads need to navigate boats down city streets. How many miles will the boats travel to cover 24 city blocks? (Remember: there is 8 city blocks per mile.)

2 If you estimated a rescue boat could travel safely at 30 miles per hour through the flooded streets, how long would a trip of 3 miles take?

DECIDE:

As a commander, you are sometimes called on to make quick decisions. You receive a report that there is a person with a serious head injury stuck on the roof of a flooded house. You look at the location on a map and have to decide quickly whether to assign a helicopter or a boat squad to the rescue.

1. A helicopter would have to fly 5 miles to rescue the victim. The helicopter travels 100 miles per hour. How much time would it take the helicopter to get to the victim?

2. A rescue boat can travel safely through the flood waters at a speed of 30 miles per hour. A rescue boat would have to travel 48 city blocks to reach the victim.
   a) How many miles is 48 city blocks?
   b) How long would it take a boat to get there?

3. Would you send a helicopter or rescue boat to save the victim? Explain your decision.

CALCULATE:

You realize your only available helicopter has broken down. The only other option you have is to send a boat squad to rescue the injured person trapped on the roof. You radio the driver of the boat. He says he should be able to travel at 60 miles per hour to get to the victim.

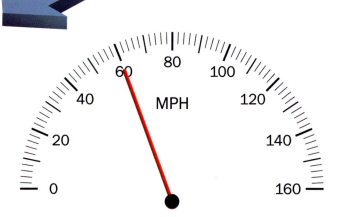

1 You know it would take 12 minutes to reach the victim traveling at 30 miles per hour. How long would it take to reach the victim 6 miles away if he boat traveled 60 miles per hour?

MATH TOOLBOX

TIME AND DISTANCE

Suppose you need to find out how long it takes a helicopter traveling at 100 miles per hour to travel 25 miles. One way of finding the time it takes to travel a certain distance is to set up a table and look for a pattern in the numbers to complete the table. Can you figure out the pattern in the table below and fill in the last missing time?

SPEED IN MILES PER HOUR	DISTANCE IN MILES	TIME IN MINUTES
100	100	60
100	75	45
100	50	30
100	25	_____

WANT TO BE A COAST GUARD COMMANDER?

1. Stay in school! A great education with a focus on science and math is the key. You used number sense and operations, measurement, and data to solve the problems in this chapter. Building on these math skills and others can help you succeed in the Coast Guard.

2. Go to your local or school library and find additional information about the Coast Guard.

3. Go to this link to learn more by reading profiles of people who have exciting careers in the Coast Guard all over the world:

www.gocoastguard.com/about-the-coast-guard/experience-the-coast-guard

CAREER 2
FIREFIGHTER

The job of a firefighter goes well beyond fighting fires. Many times duties involve responding to medical emergencies or motor vehicle accidents, and educating the public about fire safety and the use of smoke detectors.

Firefighters must be extremely fit, very brave, and well trained in the use of firefighting equipment, chemical hazards, first aid, and rescue **techniques**. Ongoing training, practice, and education is a large part of a firefighter's career. Firefighters must be prepared night and day to serve their communities. They often work night **shifts**.

Think Like a Firefighter

Firefighters use different math skills in many areas of their jobs. For example, when fighting fires, they need to know how much water can be pumped by their trucks, how far the hoses will reach, and how much **water pressure** is needed to put out a fire.

SOLVE:

1 Suppose a firefighter knows that one 30-meter hose holds about 30 liters of water. How many liters of water would one meter of hose hold?

2 If one liter of water weighs one kilogram, what is the weight of the water filling a 30-meter hose?

3 A tanker truck can carry 3,785 liters of water. What is the weight of the water carried in the tanker truck?

4 Suppose a 30-meter fire hose weighs 12 kilograms when empty, and holds 30 liters of water when full. What is the combined weight of the fire hose and the water held in it?

5 In one minute, a hose pumps 250 liters of water. In two minutes, it pumps 500 liters of water. In three minutes, it pumps 750 liters. How long will it take for the hose to pump 3,000 liters of water onto the fire? Make a table to help you look for patterns in the numbers.

FACTS:

Firefighters must learn about the patterns that fires follow. Let's look at some of the things firefighters learn. In order for a fire to burn, fuel, oxygen, and a heat source must be available. This is sometimes called the "fire triangle" because a triangle has three points, and each point in a fire triangle represents one of the three things needed to create a fire.

Firefighters put out fires by removing at least one of the three parts. They use water to lower the temperature of fuel so it won't ignite. They can also try to remove possible fuel sources, or replace oxygen with carbon dioxide—the material sprayed from a fire extinguisher.

Fires can move extremely quickly. The rate of how quickly a fire spreads depends on factors such as wind speed and the type of material that is burning. The shape of a fire changes because of the wind. A strong wind can push the flames horizontally and make the fire spread very rapidly. In a forest fire, the fire can jump from tree to tree by catching the tops of the trees. This is called crowning and can be dangerous for firefighters caught below it. A forest fire can move as quickly as 14 miles per hour.

ANALYZE:

1 List the three points of the fire triangle. What fraction of the fire triangle is each of the points?

2 You estimate the height of a fire at 100 feet and its length at 300 feet. How many times greater is its length than its height?

3 A forest fire is spreading at a rate of 12 miles per hour. A nearby town is 42 miles away. How many hours will the fire take to get to the town if the fire continues to spread at the same rate?

 DECIDE:

You are called to a cottage whose cedar roof has caught fire. Embers from the forest fire have landed on it. The cottage's owner is sleeping upstairs. You put on your **breathing apparatus** which gives you enough air for 30 minutes.

1 If you give yourself 5 minutes to enter the house and 10 minutes to reach the bedroom where the cottage owner is, how many minutes do you have to find your way back out of the building with her?

2 Suppose you weigh 165 pounds, your equipment weighs 45 pounds, and the woman being rescued weighs 135 pounds. What is the sum of your weight, the equipment you are wearing, and the woman you are carrying? What is one reason it might matter how much weight is on the floor of a burning building?

TOUGH DECISION:

You have successfully carried the woman out of the building and carefully laid her on the ground.

1. Thankfully, her breathing seems normal. She takes 6 breaths in 30 seconds. How many times did she breathe per minute? This is called her respiration.

2. You measure her **pulse** and find her heart is beating 20 times in 15 seconds. What is her heart rate in beats per minute?

The fire captain comes by to check on the rescued woman's condition. She tells you that the **paramedics** are stuck in heavy traffic, and that if the woman starts to have trouble breathing, she will call for the medical helicopter to pick her up. You write down her breathing and heart rates every 2 minutes.

TIME	BREATHING RATE PER MINUTE	HEART RATE PER MINUTE
0	12	80
2	24	92
4	36	90
6	36	110
8	40	130

3. Look at the data. Is her heart rate increasing, decreasing, or staying the same? What about her breathing rate?

4. The woman starts to cough. You know from your training that coughing and an increase in breathing rate can be signs that a person has breathed in smoke. Smoke **inhalation** is an emergency situation that requires fast action. Look at the woman's breathing rates. Do you think you should call for the helicopter? Use the data in the table to back up your decision.

NAME: Bill Reiach
POSITION: Captain of Mississauga Fire and Emergency Services (Retired)

How do you use math in your career?

The most important use of math has to do with getting water from a fire hydrant to the fire. There needs to be a certain amount of water pressure to put the fire out, and the amount needs constant calculations when fighting fires.

Hand-held hoses used to fight fires carry the water from the hydrant, along the hose, then shoot water out their nozzles. Water loses pressure the longer it travels through hoses. The amount of pressure loss depends on the size of the hose and the number of pieces (lengths) of hose. Firefighters have to calculate the amount of pressure lost so that they can pump the water faster to make up for this loss.

It gets more complicated when fighting fires that are higher than the ground. Water loses pressure for every meter of height. Firefighters have to estimate how high the hose is being raised, and figure out how much pressure is being lost. They have to pump the water faster to make up for this loss. So, as the fire gets bigger or smaller, firefighters need to constantly calculate changing water pressure and make adjustments.

PATTERNS IN NUMBERS

When using a set of numbers to make a decision, it helps to look for patterns in the numbers. Ask yourself if the numbers seem to be changing as if they are following a rule. Do you see steady change or are the numbers staying approximately the same? If the numbers in a table are changing, are they increasing or decreasing? If so, by how much? Do the numbers increase or decrease by the same amount? If they do, you can find the rule the numbers are following. Then you can use the rule to back up your decision.

This could be you!

WANT TO BE A FIREFIGHTER?

1. **Stay in school!** You have used tables, patterns, and estimations in this chapter. This kind of mathematical thinking is an important part of this amazing career.

2. **Ask your teacher** to try to arrange a visit from your local fire department so your class can ask questions about how to become a firefighter.

3. **When you are old enough,** you may **consider applying for the** volunteer fire department **in your community**.

CAREER 3

POLICE OFFICER

Police officers are in charge of enforcing the law, investigating crimes, and protecting the community. Officers are trained in police driving techniques, first aid, using weapons, and the use of force. An officer must be physically fit, be knowledgeable of the law, know how to handle difficult situations, and always remain calm.

Police officers are important parts of their communities. They make sure that communities are safe places to live.

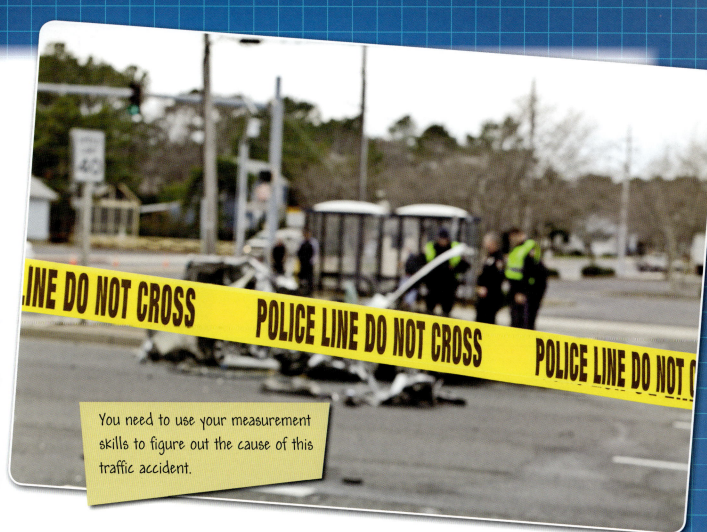

You need to use your measurement skills to figure out the cause of this traffic accident.

Think Like a Police Officer

Suppose you are a police officer. While you are out on patrol, the **dispatcher** comes over your patrol car's radio to tell you there is a traffic accident ahead. You put on your lights and siren, and speed to the scene.

Down the highway, you come across the accident scene. One vehicle has crashed into the rear end of another. When you get there, you jump out of your patrol car leaving the flashing lights on. Other police officers are already there directing traffic. You comfort one of the injured people until the paramedics arrive.

Now, your **investigation** begins. Skid marks made by tires can be seen on the road trailing behind one of the cars. You carefully take pictures of the marks, then get out a tape measure and accurately find their lengths. The length of a skid mark can be used to estimate the speed the car was going when it made the skid marks.

SOLVE:

1 There are 12 inches in one foot. If a skid mark is 10 feet long, how many inches is that?

2 The same skid mark is the shape of a long rectangle. If the skid mark is 9 inches wide, what is the total area of the mark?

3 How many inches is 7 feet 11 inches?

FACTS:

You interview the drivers at the accident scene to learn more about the events leading up to the accident. Police use interviews to help draw a picture to reconstruct the accident. You label the vehicle in front Car A and the vehicle that was following behind Car B.

The driver of Car A states she was driving along the highway at 55 miles per hour. A deer came out of the woods and walked onto the highway ahead of her. She said she carefully applied the brakes and slowed down to let the deer get off the road. That was when her car was hit from behind by Car B.

The driver of Car B states that he was driving along the road at a speed of 60 miles per hour when Car A suddenly slowed down. He says he slammed on the brakes but could not avoid hitting her.

The maximum speed limit of the highway is 60 miles per hour. To help the investigation, you do some calculations in order to find out how far Car B traveled in one second.

1
a) You know there are 60 minutes in one hour. If a vehicle is traveling 60 miles per hour, how many miles does the vehicle travel in one minute?
b) Since a mile equals 5,280 feet, how many feet does the vehicle go in one minute?
c) Knowing there are 60 seconds in a minute, how many feet would the driver of Car B travel in one second?

2 If the driver of Car B was distracted and took his eyes off the road for three seconds, how far would his car travel in that time?

ANALYZE:

During an accident investigation, police officers collect clues in order to figure out the cause of the crash. By recreating the movements of the cars just before the accident, they may be able prove who is at fault for the accident. The table below contains information about the distance in feet traveled every $1/10$ of a second if a car's speed is 60 miles per hour. Use the pattern in the table to fill in the blanks, assuming the pattern stays the same.

TIME IN SECONDS	DISTANCE TRAVELED IN FEET
0.1	8.8
0.2	17.6
0.3	26.4
0.4	_____
0.5	_____

ESTIMATE:

As you saw in the situation on page 26, a car traveling at highway speeds can travel a long way in a short amount of time. A car traveling on a highway at 60 miles per hour moves 88 feet per second.

1. One of the rules of the road is that you must leave enough distance between your car and the car in front of you. This allows you to come to a safe stop if the car in front of you slows down or stops suddenly. A basic rule of thumb is that you should stay a minimum of two car lengths behind the car in front of you. If the average car is 15 feet long, estimate the number of feet in two car lengths.

2. Was Car B traveling at a safe distance behind Car A? Is there enough **data** to support your thinking? Explain.

TOUGH DECISION:

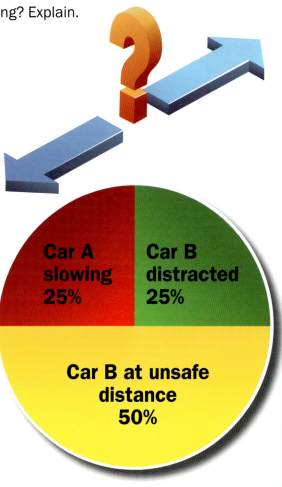

At the end of the investigation, an investigator must decide which car was at fault, or if both cars were partially at fault, for the accident.

A pie chart is a good way to show numbers in a visual form. Suppose you determine that the accident was caused by several factors. You give each factor a percentage according to its importance: 50% due to Car B leaving an unsafe distance between cars, 25% due to distracted driving by Car B, and 25% due to Car A having to slow down suddenly to avoid the deer. These conclusions are in the form of a pie chart at right. By total percentage, which car do you conclude was most responsible?

PIE CHARTS

There are a number of ways to illustrate partial amounts of the same whole. One method is to draw a pie shape and shade each portion different colors.

For example, if one car was ¼ responsible for the accident and the other car was ¾ responsible, you could show a pie shape cut into quarters with ¼ colored red and ¾ colored blue. The goal of an accident investigation is to determine who is at fault, and if fault is shared, how much damage each driver is responsible for.

WANT TO BE A POLICE OFFICER?

1. Stay in school! A great education with a focus on science and math is the key. A high school diploma is a minimum requirement. As you can see, police investigators use math a lot in their work.

2. Go to your school guidance counselor or local library and ask about police force training and careers.

This could be you!

Learning More

Websites

This website focuses on firefighters and their roles in our communities. Information covers tools, equipment, and fire safety tips: www.explainthatstuff.com/firefighting.html

This website focuses on police officers and includes information about required skills and training, different work environments, and the outlook for future jobs in the field: www.bls.gov/ooh/protective-service/police-and-detectives.htm

This website features an interview with a firefighter. Content includes an explanation of the math needed for the job: http://bedtimemath.org/fighting-fire-with-numbers/

Books

Clemson, Wendy & David Clemson. *Firefighters to the Rescue*. Real-World Math Series: Tick-Tock Books, 2013.

Herweck, Diana. *All In A Day's Work: Police Officer*. Time For Kids Readers: Teacher Created Materials, 2013.

McDonnell. *Coast Guard*. US Military Forces: Gareth Stevens, 2011.

ANSWERS:

Career 1: Coast Guard Commander

Solve: 1) 90 personnel ÷ 30 squads = 3 people, 2) a) 90 × $\frac{1}{3}$ = 30 people with first aid,
b) 30 squads ÷ 30 first aid people = 1 person per squad,
3) a) Area = 12 × 10 = 120 square miles,
b) Perimeter = 10 +12 + 10 + 12 = 44 miles.

Analyze: 1) 24 blocks ÷ (8 blocks x 1 mile) = 3 miles.
2) 1 hour = 60 minutes, 60 min. ÷ 30 miles = 2 min. for every mile,
2 min. x 3 miles = 6 min. A 3-mile trip would take 6 minutes.

Decide: 1) 60 min. ÷ 100 miles = 0.6 min. per mile, 0.6 min. x 5 miles = 3 minutes
2) a) 48 blocks ÷ (8 blocks x 1 mile) = 6 miles.
b) 60 min. ÷ 30 miles = 2 min. per mile, 2 min. x 6 miles = 12 minutes
3) I would send the helicopter because it would only take 3 minutes instead of 12 minutes to get to the injured victim.

Calculate: 1) 60 min. ÷ 60 miles = 1 min. every mile, 1 min. x 6 miles = 6 min.
It would take 6 minutes to reach the victim going 60 miles per hour.

Math Toolbox: The pattern in the table shows it takes 15 minutes to travel every 25 miles.
The last missing time is 15.

Glossary

breathing apparatus A device worn by rescue workers that contains breathable air

carbon dioxide A gas that does not burn. It is sprayed from fire extinguishers on the base of a fire to push away the oxygen that feeds it.

data Facts or information

dispatcher The person who determines which workers will do which jobs

fuel Materials that can burn

heat source The place where heat comes from; for example, a burning match

hypothermic Below normal body temperature

ignite To catch fire

inhalation The act of inhaling, or drawing air (or smoke) into the lungs

investigation To find out the facts about something

oil rigs Structures built on water from which oil wells are drilled and oil is extracted

oxygen Relating to fire; a chemical element that contributes to starting and supporting a fire

paramedic A professional who provides medical help before a person gets to a hospital

pulse The number of times a person's heart beats per minute

reconstruct To rebuild or re-create from given information

shifts Periods of work according to a schedule

squad A small group of people who perform their duties together

technique A way of doing something

units Groups within a larger organization, defined by the kind of work they do

volunteer fire department A unit of non-professional volunteers who can be called on by fire departments in emergencies

water pressure The measure of force applied to water to push it forward

---

ANSWERS CONTINUED
Career 2: Firefigher
Solve: 1) 30 liters ÷ 30 meters = 1 liter of water in every 1 meter of hose.
2) 30 liters × 1 kilogram = 30 kg. The weight of the water filling a 30-meter hose is 30 kg.
3) 3,785 liters × 1 kilogram = 3,785 kg of water
4) 12 kg hose + 30 kg of water = 42 kg altogether
5) The pattern shows that the hose pumps 250 liters every minute. To pump 3,000 liters of water, it will take 3,000 liters ÷ 250 liters per minute = 12 minutes.

Index

area 8, 24
distance (miles)
  9, 10, 11, 12, 13,
  18, 25, 26, 27
fractions 8, 18, 28
length 8, 18, 23,
  24, 27
patterns 13, 16,
  17, 20, 26
perimeter 8
speed (mph) 10,
  11, 12, 13, 17, 18,
  23, 25, 26, 27
time 10, 11, 12,
  13, 18, 19, 25,
  26, 27
weight 16, 18
width 8, 24

Author's Bio:
Rick admires and appreciates the brave men and women who risk their lives every day to protect and serve our communities. They are his heroes! Rick loves learning about science and math and has the best job in the world for him—a teacher.

ANSWERS CONTINUED

Career 2: Firefigher

Analyze: 1) The three points are fuel, oxygen, and heat. Each of these points is ⅓ of the fire triangle.
    2) 300 feet long ÷ 100 feet high = 3 times greater length than height,
    3) 42 miles ÷ 12 mph = 3.5 hours.

Decide: 1) 30 minutes - 5 - 10 = 15 minutes of oxygen left to get out of the house
    2) 165 + 45 + 135 = 345 pounds. The building's floor may be weakened by the fire and not be able to hold very much weight.

Tough Decision: 1) respiration = 10 breaths in 30 seconds × 2 = 20 breaths per minute;
    2) pulse = 20 beats in 15 seconds × 4 = 80 beats per minute, 3) Breathing rate and heart rate are both increasing; 4) Breaths are increasing rapidly, so call for help.

Career 3: Police Officer

Solve: 1) 12 inches x 10 feet = 120 inches long, 2) area = 120 inches x 9 inches = 1,080 square inches, 3) (7 feet × 12 inches) + 11 inches = 95 inches.

Facts: 1) 60 miles ÷ 60 mph = 1 mile traveled per minute;
    5,280 feet × one minute = 5,280 feet traveled in one minute;
    5,280 feet per minute ÷ 60 seconds = 88 feet traveled per second.
    2) 3 seconds × 88 feet per second = 264 feet in three seconds.

Analyze: The pattern in the table shows the car traveled 8.8 feet every 0.1 seconds. The car would have traveled 26.4 + 8.8 = 35.2 feet in 0.4 seconds, and 35.2 + 8.8 = 44 feet in 0.5 seconds.

Estimate: 1) 2 x 15 feet = 30 feet between cars;
    2) Car B was probably not a safe distance from Car A since the cars collided. We don't really have enough data to support this because we don't know the distance between the cars.

Tough Decision: Car A = 25% responsible, and Car B = 50% + 25% = 75% responsible. Car B has a higher percentage of responsibility for the accident.